The
MLM
BINARY
PLAN

Also by

Ray H. Duncan

The MLM ROAD MAP

The
MLM
BINARY
PLAN

A Comprehensive Look at Network Marketing's Most Controversial Distributor Compensation Plan

By
Ray H. Duncan

Double Diamond Publishing
New Orleans, LA

Library of Congress Catalog-in-Publication Data
Duncan, Ray H.
The Binary Plan, A Comprehensive Look at Network Marketing's Most Controversial Distributor Compensation Plan / by Ray H. Duncan.
1st Edition, 2000
p.   cm.
ISBN 1-929746-01-6
1. Binary 2. Network Marketing 3. MLM
Library of Congress Catalog Card Number: 99-091137

CONTENTS

DEDICATION

To Bill Worden,

Who encouraged me to get the idea off the ground, provided suggestions, and convinced me that this book would be a valuable reference for everyone involved in the network marketing industry.

To Peter and Andrew Spary of The MultiSoft Corporation,

For their friendship and extensive knowledge of the binary compensation plan.

Ray H. Duncan, 2000

FOREWORD

During my fifteen-year career as a full-time network marketer, I have built and developed several highly successful and long-term downlines with network marketing companies. A few years ago I joined a company and was introduced to the Binary Compensation Plan. While remarkably different from the stair-step plans I had been so successful with, the Binary proved to be the most successful of all, producing over a six-figure income within the first year. While the Binary proved to be the most challenging plan I had ever worked, it also proved to be the most successful and produced a top income for me in a shorter amount of time.

If this book had been available at that time, I am certain I would have achieved a much higher degree of success, as would have members of my downline. This book has possibly the information most needed in our industry when it comes to companies with Binary compensation plans. Ray answers the pertinent questions while dispelling the myths and misconceptions of this newcomer to the network marketing industry. Now, those working a network marketing company with a Binary compensation plan will have the opportunity to use the information presented in this book to build their organizations.

I feel extremely fortunate for the opportunity to work with Ray on the development of this book, and I know that the information contained herein will be of immense value to all those working with the Binary Compensation Plan.

Bill Worden, MBA
New Orleans, LA

INTRODUCTION

This book will explain aspects of the binary marketing plan that may not have been previously explained. The reader is also referred to another book by the same author, The MLM ROAD MAP, which explains a simple and easily duplicated system of building a well-proportioned downline sales organization.

One of the hard truths in network marketing is that many people do not go to work with the commitment or dedication that it requires to become successful. I worked as Chief Operating Officer with two network marketing companies and was National Sales and Marketing Director with a third. It was my job to find out just what it took for our company(s) to be successful. I found that no matter how quickly we shipped products, how soon the commission checks were sent, or how great the literature and products were, the success of the company ALWAYS depended on the field of distributors and the design of the distributor compensation plan..

You see, network marketing is quite different from conventional sales. A store has a certain fixed number of salespeople. They stock the shelves and make the products available to the masses. When an employee quits or is fired, the management replaces that worker. In network marketing companies, the employees are independent distributors. When a distributor quits, there is no management to appoint a replacement. The field of independent distributors must be structured and managed internally; otherwise, when enough people drop out, the company will cease to sell its products and soon be closed.

So network marketing companies must follow a plan of action and keep the independent distributors working with each other to promote the products.

The multilevel sales plans arose in the 1950s and have since been re-engineered as much as the modern day automobile. In a multilevel sales plan, distributors not only earn money on their own direct sales, but they also earn override commissions on the sales of their recruited salespeople and all downline members linked by sponsorship.

In the early multilevel programs, some distributors earned the right to purchase directly from the company and supply their downline distributors with products and sometimes commission earnings. Most of these companies started when computer technology was in its early stages, and it was difficult to manage all the downline information and commission payouts.

With advances in computer technology, the need for some key distributors to act as a go-between has disappeared, and the distributor compensation plans have been greatly enhanced.

These enhancements have evolved into several general "TYPES" of distributor compensation plans. They are:

UNILEVEL

The unilevel is one of the earliest forms of network marketing compensation structures. These plans allow distributors to sponsor an unlimited number of first generation (or level) distributors. Compensation is earned from the first five to eight levels with five being the most common. Fixed and sometimes varying percentages are paid on sales volume on each pay level. It is the total of these percentages that ultimately determines the maximum payout to the field of distributors. Some unilevel plans have roll-ups, compression, and/or infinity bonuses. This allows top distributors to qualify for deeper level commissions until downline leaders achieve higher recognition and also qualify for deeper commissions. Some current pay plans also incorporate an "infinity bonus." This can be misleading, as infinity is only to the next distributor with equal qualification. Volume accumulates through the end of the month, and generally checks are issued once per month. There are also companies offering "Matching Bonuses" based on the performance of personally sponsored distributors.

STAIR-STEP BREAK-A-WAY

The stair-step break-a-way plan is an unlimited width plan, allowing distributors to sponsor an unlimited number of people on their front line (first generation). Many stair-step break-a-way plans have width requirements to reach volume in depth and large quotas and group volume requirements. These plans are loaded with individual qualifiers that distributors must earn in order to derive higher commissions in the plan. Usually they pay five to seven levels deep, and commissions are earned from fixed percentage amounts paid on sales volume. It is the total of these percentages according to the limited levels that determines the maximum payout.

The break-a-way plan derived its name because of the fact that when a distributor reaches a certain volume level, his/her entire group breaks away from the commission group. Some plans allow you to continue to earn a small percentage of the sales volume that this break-a-way group attains. Many distributors coined the phrase "Break-a-way is Take-a-way" because their commissions either stopped or diminished after the break-a-way occurred.

MATRIX

Matrix distributor compensation plans limit first level placement, allowing you to sponsor only a certain number of people on your front line. Each level has the same limit as first level placement, thus forcing your organization to grow to a specified structure. Distributors are also restricted from sponsoring outside the matrix, and there is a limit to depth. Once the level is filled, the next distributor will be automatically placed on the next available level. Commissions are derived from a fixed percentage paid on sales occurring on each level. The percentage can also vary , depending on the level. It is the total of these percentages that sets the maximum payout.

The matrix plan usually pays monthly. These plans sometimes incorporate daily "fast start" bonuses. At first glance, matrix earnings can appear very lucrative; however, one must build an entire matrix in order to earn these amounts. Because the greatest amount of income is usually derived from the last three levels, these earnings are not obtainable by most network marketers. Width placement limits are generally from two to five, and depth is limited from five to twelve. The allure of the matrix pay plan has always been the "spillover." This occurs when upline representatives sponsor more than their required quota. Since the industry average for personal sponsorship is below three distributors, worthwhile spillover in the matrix plans rarely ever happens.

BINARY PLANS

The binary compensation structure is basically an unlimited depth, two-wide matrix. You can place only two people on your first level. Everyone else goes beneath those people. Binary commissions are earned by accumulating a specified amount of sales volume. This sales volume may accumulate over an unlimited period of time. There is no depth limit in the binary plan. Every sale will accumulate toward the specified amount of sales volume requirement. The number of levels between you and a given recruit is not important. The factor determining whether you get a commission from that person is not what level he/she is on, but rather how much commissionable sales volume is generated in the levels between you and that person.

Each tracking position is divided into a left and a right, and the binary plans issue commission earnings based on a pre-defined match of sales volume. There are no group volume requirements or quotas. Binary plans require legs to be balanced. Average payout is 10% on unlimited depth. Some plans pay out as much as 20% on unlimited levels if all legs are balanced. Because of product costs, there are variations from plan to plan. Some binary plans pay on equal volume matches (50/50), meaning that volume needs to balance on each side to receive a commission check that week. Other plans have a 1/3-2/3 split, meaning you can have up to 66% of your volume on the

12

strong side and still match with 33% on the weak leg.

All plans have a daily or weekly limit. This daily or weekly limit is pre-defined in the tracking software and is the ultimate key which sets the maximum distributor payout.

Unilevel, stair-step break-a-ways, and matrix plans pay commissions on all purchases that occur through a specified maximum number of levels (generally five to twelve), regardless of how small or large a cash amount that might be. Binary plans turn that around. They pay on all sales that occur through a specified maximum dollar amount, regardless of how many levels away they accumulate from.

As you can see, all forms of network marketing compensation plans are restricted by design to allow a certain "maximum" percentage of sales to be paid to the field of distributors. Good network marketers can earn from any commission plan. Some plans have more requirements than others and are slightly more difficult for the inexperienced distributor.

In my opinion, the binary compensation plan is the simplest form of compensation. If independent distributors can be taught to duplicate themselves and teach others to do the same, they can achieve success! There is nothing easier than building only two legs.

Success with the binary plan of distributor compensation does take hard work, a complete understanding of its mechanics, and the sponsoring of people that will go to work!

As long as there are more than two network marketing companies offering income opportunities, there will be new innovative changes to distributor pay plans. The binary does require people to go to work to earn their commission checks. There is no free ride to the commission check - - a fact that has brought criticism from certain distributors in our industry.

This book was written because I grew to recognize the binary form of distributor compensation to be the ultimate **CASH MACHINE** for both distributor and company. The binary is the fastest building form of distributor compensation ever designed. Binary marketing plans do not focus on how much percent is paid out in each level, or how many people you must develop to earn a check. Rather, they focus the attention on how many sales must be recorded on each side of a tracking center to earn a commission check. There are no set levels or limitations. The binary allows distributors to accumulate sales from their entire organization for compensation. Some forms focus on sales volume rather than individual sales. Either way, the binary plan tells distributors exactly what needs to happen in order to earn a commission check.

CHAPTER ONE

Myths & Misconceptions

Perhaps no other Network Marketing Distributor Compensation Plan has been the subject of so many Myths or Misconceptions than the Binary Plan.

The most common myths are:

"I had a runaway leg."
"Binary plans are illegal."
"Binary plans are only for the company."
"You can't control growth."
"AGs don't like the binary plans, so any company using a binary will surely be shut down."
"Binaries don't work."
"I don't like binaries."

You may have heard many other negative comments about the binary plans, but the most common comment I hear is:
"I don't like binaries."

It has been said that a myth is a story that is shared by a group of people who find their most important meanings in it; is a story believed to have been composed in the past about an event in the past, or more rarely, in the future; an event that continues to have meaning in the present because it is remembered.

According to this definition, many of the binary "stories" should be included in the category of myth. Myths play a significant role in the personal and corporate life of each culture; they serve a wide range of psychological and social functions. The myths in Network Marketing are no different. Our focus, therefore, is on their effects and functions within our industry.

Before you believe myths (or stories) about the binary compensation plan, you should investigate their origins, and you will find that they are rooted in prejudice, superstition, or hearsay.

The purpose of this book is to help skeptical networkers emerge from ignorance of the MLM Binary Distributor Compensation Plan and free their minds of mythology and wrong concepts. Resistance to change can lead to wrong thinking; but when you open up your mind and learn to understand the binary, you will begin to see in a graphic way why it works so well. My intention is to give you the know-how to make it work successfully for you, as it has for hundreds of others.

What we must all recognize is that the entire world and everything in it undergoes constant change. Unless we are open minded enough to recognize change and improvement, we will certainly be left behind! Please do not allow yourself to be left behind!

"Nothing in this world is so powerful as an idea whose time has come."

. . . Victor Hugo

CHAPTER TWO

Facts

If you look closely, you will find many different forms of the Binary Compensation Plan. Network Marketing companies tend to create their own improvements to compensation plans in order to be a little different, with the goal of attracting distributors with a new compensation plan twist.

The basic Binary plan is binary by nature, meaning it has two parts.

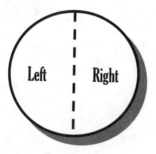

All binary tracking centers have a left and a right side. It is this division that gives the binary its name. Your commission earnings are based on sales made in both of these legs. These sales are generally tracked by sophisticated corporate software and programmed to pay commissions based on certain qualifications.

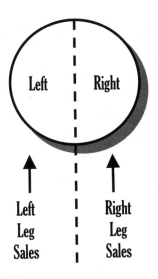

Left | Right

↑ | ↑

Left | Right
Leg | Leg
Sales | Sales

Please understand that NO distributor compensation plans pay to infinity. They all MUST have a limit.

Think of a binary commission calculation like you are filling up two buckets with water. When each bucket is full, you earn a commission check and empty the water out. You start filling the buckets up with water again and when they are full, you earn another commission check. As you develop other distributors on your left and right sides, they are helping you to fill your buckets. All the work that everyone in your downline sales organization does helps to fill your buckets.

Some plans allow you to earn commission checks in different stages. In other words, they give you smaller buckets to pour into the larger one. Every time you fill each of the smaller buckets, you earn a commission check; but when the larger bucket has been filled, you will have earned the maximum earnings for that pay period, and you must wait until the next pay cycle to earn more commissions.

EXAMPLE: XYZ MLM Company has a binary compensation plan that will pay commissions up to $5,000 per week per tracking center. Commissions are earned in increments of $250. So it is possible to earn twenty individual checks each week or a combination of up to twenty increments on one check.

In this example, XYZ MLM Company has set its pay percentage for the field (distributor force) to allow the maximum pay to reach $5,000 per week. This is no different than a stair-step break-a-way plan that limits earnings to levels. The binary plan allows all sales occurring below your tracking number to accumulate toward your commissionable earnings, rather than ONLY those sales that occur in a specified number of levels.

The big difference between the binary plan and the unilevel or stair-step break-a-way plan is the number of legs you must develop. Most of the stair-step break-a-way plans require you to develop at least five legs in width in order for you to earn from sales five or six levels in depth. Even the most stubborn binary opponents must admit that building five legs requires more work and diversification than building only two.

When you build and develop more than two legs in a program, you are spending less time and attention with your personally sponsored distributors than you would if you were building only two. Let's say you devote twenty hours each week to your MLM opportunity. In the following example you have an organization that is five wide, and you have allotted four hours every week to help each of your front line, or personally sponsored, distributors.

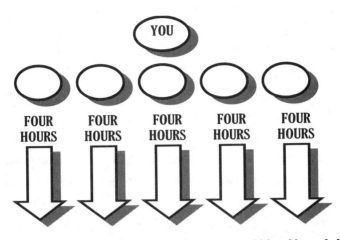

Now if you were working only two legs, you would be able to dedicate ten hours per leg, thus giving each person in your organization a much better allotment of your time.

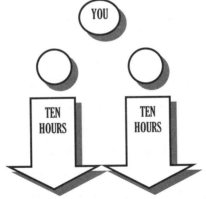

Even those opposed to the binary must realize that time management is a key element in developing a linked-by-sponsorship downline sales organization; that dividing their time between only two legs will be better time management than five or more!

Another BIG advantage to the binary compensation plan is the additional placement made by sponsoring more than two distributors. If you are building one tracking center, then all distributors you sponsor after your first two must be placed either in your left leg or your right leg. This placement will be helping everyone in that leg that this contract links to. This is an advantage of the binary that other forms of compensation plans do not have. If you were working an unlimited width plan, you would be placing your additional personally sponsored distributors on your first level. Here they would not be helping anyone but you, and you would have to adjust your time allotment to include them, thus taking time away from your other distributors. So in the binary, each time you sponsor a new distributor, you are helping everyone in your downline above this placement. What could be better?

Now let's dispel some of the myths:

MYTH #1: "I had a runaway leg."

This term is used to describe a left or right leg that has outgrown the other by a considerable amount. While this may be alarming to some distributors, the smart networker would consider a runaway leg to be a blessing or a gift. Having a runaway leg allows you to know exactly where you must work and develop volume in order to qualify for a commission check.

Let's say, for example, that your company paid a $250 commission each time you accumulated $1,000 in sales on the left and the right legs of your binary tracking number, and you had a runaway leg that was producing $10,000 in sales each week. YOU WOULD ONLY HAVE TO DEVELOP SALES ON THE OTHER SIDE TO EARN A COMMISSION CHECK! What is wrong with that?

22

NOTHING is WRONG! If you can't make sales or develop other distributors that CAN make sales, then you are in the wrong business. A runaway leg requires you to work ONLY ONE leg to get paid! Now you could devote the entire twenty hours to developing sales and new distributors
in ONLY ONE LEG!

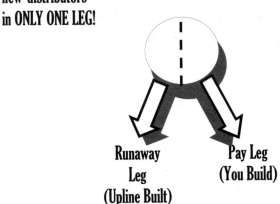

Runaway
Leg
(Upline Built)

Pay Leg
(You Build)

MYTH #2: "Binary plans are illegal."

The common myth or misconception that the binary plan is illegal is an unfair statement, and there is absolutely no substantial reason for the myth. If we looked at what possibly started this myth, we would find that three of the biggest failed companies in the last 10 years had binary plans. They all attracted tremendous numbers of people, but their fates were cast from the start: not closed because of the binary plan as the myth might imply, but for basic operational reasons.

One company with over 100,000 people was closed by authorities who challenged it as a recruiting scheme. It was closed because that is exactly what it was! It was a recruiting scheme that paid commissions on unfulfilled contracts for undelivered products. The binary plan never entered the picture with the regulatory agencies. It would have been illegal with any plan, binary or otherwise, so it was closed.

A second company was also challenged as a recruiting scheme, and close to a half-million people were involved. It was forced into bankruptcy after the legal objections stopped the cash flow, but the binary plan was never challenged. The problem arose from a sponsoring strategy that made it look like a recruiting scheme, and that sponsoring strategy drew legal challenges that led to its demise.

If the company had overcome the cash flow problem and changed its recruiting and sponsoring strategies, then it could still be in business today. Actually, it was allowed to continue business with the binary after changing its recruiting and sponsoring strategies; but damaged by little or no cash flow, it could not continue. The binary plan used by this company was never challenged.

A third and a fourth were closed. The latter was one of the largest binary companies, with several hundred thousand people registered as representatives. Its demise was not because of legal challenges, but by problems derived from poor management. The problems did not reflect on its binary plan, so the binary wasn't the culprit. The shame is that the company could be in business today with the same plan if it could have had better management.

Two of these three companies had legal problems and all had binary plans, and that's the basis for the legal mythology. "The prophets of doom," out of ignorance, blamed the binary. There are several other large companies successfully using the binary plan and have done so for at least five years without any legal problems associated with their binary distributor plans. All have about 100,000 people. Many newer companies today also use the binary system without any legal complications. In fact, the latest rumor mill is calling the other more conventional plans "DINOSAURS!"

MYTH #3: "Binary plans are only for the company."

All companies MUST make a profit, and distributors should hope that their company does; otherwise, they won't be around very long. When someone makes the above statement, obviously they are not doing the work to earn a check and are laying the blame on the company or compensation plan, rather than on themselves and their own efforts.

Most MLM companies pay as much to the field of independent distributors as they can. The binary plans are no exceptions. Rather than trying to figure out what percentage a company pays out, the distributor should figure out how many sales he or she needs to develop each week to earn his or her desired commission level.

For comparison, let's look at three of the largest stair-step break-a-way plans and compare the actual distributor payout to that of several large binary companies.

First is Herbalife, a giant in the industry with a stair-step break-a-way. According to the company's annual report filed in 1997, Herbalife's gross sales were $1.2 billion. $568 million was paid in "distributor allowances on product purchases," or rebates, so net sales were $632 million. From net sales the company paid $185 million in "royalty overrides." A quick calculation shows that Herbalife paid 29% in commissions.

The 1996 annual report of another stair-step break-a-way company, Reliv International, shows "sales at suggested retail" of $61 million. Reliv paid $20 million in "allowances on product purchases," or rebates, leaving net sales of $41 million. From net sales, Reliv International paid $14 million in "distributor royalties and commissions," so Reliv paid 34% in commissions.

NSA is another giant with a stair-step break-a-way commission plan. Their annual report shows a "percentage of net revenues" paid in 'dealer/distributor commissions and allowances' of 20.69%.

Now that we know the payout of three companies with break-a-way plans, we can compare payout for the binary in the annual reports of two publicly traded companies with binary compensation plans.

USANA, a 6-year old company with a binary plan, showed $85 million in net sales in its annual report for 1997. From those net sales Usana paid $40 million in "distributor incentives," which calculates to 47% in commissions.

Market America, a 6-year old company with a binary distributor compensation plan, showed 1997 net sales of $66 million in its annual report and paid "commissions" of $30 million, so Market America paid 45% in commissions.

In review, the stair-step break-a-way plan has NSA at 21%, Herbalife at 29%, and Reliv at 34%. The binary plan has Market America at 45% and Usana at 47%.

Which plan has the highest payout percentage? THE BINARY! Which plan pays the company more? THE STAIR-STEP BREAK-A-WAY! Which plan pays the distributors more? Which is the fairest? THE BINARY! The binary has the highest payout, the stair-step break-a-way has the most breakage. The stair-step break-a-way pays the COMPANY MORE, and the binary pays the DISTRIBUTORS MORE!

MYTH #4: "You can't control growth."

Why would any distributor wish to control the growth of his/her sales organization? LET IT GROW, LET IT GROW, LET IT GROW!

The above statement is usually associated with the statement, "I can't match the volume." That only means that the distributor can't build or develop sales.

MYTH #5: "AGs don't like the binary plans, so any company using a binary will surely be shut down."

I have never been able to understand this myth or statement. Many distributors who work a binary plan do not understand it. Attorney Generals do not participate in network marketing companies or understand the binary, nor do they regulate HOW a company pays their representatives. Most are concerned with a company NOT shipping products, NOT paying commissions, deceptive trade practices, income claims, or other ethical matters.

The binary plan has been mistaken as "guilty by association." Bad reports have surfaced; and after a review of case histories, research has found that in every case these programs were investigated, fined, or shut down based on criteria other than the compensation plan. The binary plan WAS NOT the reason or criteria that these companies were forced to dissolve.

If an attorney general understands the binary marketing plan and the principles associated with it, he/she will quickly see that the binary plan DOES NOT OFFER A FREE RIDE to distributors. It is not a pyramid system. Commissions are based solely on an individual's sales and those of his/her downline.

In the binary plan, there are no free rides. The distributors that go to work, make sales, and sponsor new distributors are the ones that earn commission checks. The distributors who take a position and sit back and wait for the commissions to start coming are the ones who usually complain that the plan doesn't work because they "never earn commissions!"

If there ever were a distributor compensation plan that should be given an A+ by Attorney Generals' offices, it should be the 50/50 binary compensation program paying commissions based solely on SALES of company products.

MYTH #6: "Binaries don't work, or binaries don't work for the little distributor."

The truth is that binary compensation DOES WORK, and it works very effectively FOR THE PEOPLE WHO WORK IT! People that do not understand the binary system, or those who are not capable of developing other distributors or outside sales, usually make these statements.

Many involved in this industry use the term "little distributors" quite a lot. If they are referring to people that are new to the business, then they should spend the time with their new distributors training and helping them succeed. The binary compensation system is the easiest system for anyone to build and develop. After all, you have to sponsor only two distributors (one on the left and one on the right), then help these distributors to sponsor two each! By helping each person when they enter a sales group, this myth can be dispelled very easily!

MYTH #7: "I don't like binaries."

This is a statement made either by someone who doesn't understand how the binary plan works, or by someone who was working a binary plan and could not recruit or make sales. The reason I say this is because the binary is the easiest and fastest building structure. Once people really understand how the binary plan works and how to build and structure, they usually rescind their statement. To dispel this myth with the person spreading it, you must first find out exactly what he or she does not like about the binary plan. Since all binary plans are NOT exactly the same, there may be a legitimate reason for someone to make this statement. After you are armed with the facts WHY he/she does not like the binary, you can explain how your company's plan works. Recently, I visited with a prospect that professed to dislike binary plans. In fact, his first comment to me was:

"If it is a binary, I don't even want to look at it."

So I asked him what he disliked about a binary, and he started telling me all of the above. I was persistent and ask him directly: "Do you like having to build more than two legs to earn commissions?" His answer was "NO." I then asked him, "Do you prefer to earn commissions only on a few levels of the organization you are building, rather than collect commissionable volume from your entire organization?" His answer was "NO." Then I asked him, "If your upline created half of your commission check each week for you, would you cash it?" His answer was "YES."

I stood back and said, "I thought you said you did not like binaries." Then he said, "It's not me, but my people. They just never seem to earn from the binaries. There is always volume they don't get paid on." I said, "The problem is not in the binary, but in your people. They either do not understand how the binary plan works, or they are not working your program and usually blame the pay structure for their failure. You either need to give each person some training on the binary and show them how to build for commissions, or find new people that are willing to go to work."

BENEFITS OF THE BINARY PLAN

Binary plans have many overlooked benefits.

BINARIES ARE NOT MULTILEVEL. In a binary, "levels" are irrelevant. The term is used ONLY in describing the location of a participant in the structure. In a binary, a person could have one leg which is only a few levels deep and another leg which is many hundred levels deep, and it is possible to maintain balanced volume if the undeveloped leg has more high volume producers (better salespersons). This situation would not be as profitable in a multilevel plan.

If one has created a "runaway leg," he/she has actually created a very fortunate situation! To experts of binary marketing, a runaway leg is a great advantage, not a problem! If you have one leg that far outperforms your other leg, you are actually fortunate because your job is half done for you. It is because the runaway leg is so strong that one can concentrate on the undeveloped leg. This concept is often misunderstood by those who compare the binary to multilevel marketing. This allows you to concentrate your efforts in building one leg.

In a binary, the upline is far less likely to compete with the downline for the same people because the system requires depth, not width. In multilevel, one has to build wide because MLM plans tend to penalize when one places high volume producers under low volume producers. However, in a binary, one is actually better off placing high volume producers under low volume producers because it motivates everyone and doesn't penalize you. In fact, it creates a built-in support system. Many of the people you sponsor would be placed "Front Line" to you in other plans. Because you only build two legs and there are no depth limitations, the binary forces you to place these new recruits under your older ones, thus helping strengthen everyone above. Other plans also do not encourage people in the upline to build under those in the downline because the compensation systems penalize distributors for giving away their recruits.

WEEKLY PAY - The majority of distributors in network marketing have been conditioned to receiving "PAY CHECKS" on a weekly or bi-weekly basis, not once a month. Most people working full-time or relying on a monthly commission check from a conventional MLM pay plan are forced to change the way they handle their finances. The binary is usually figured in a weekly commissions calculation. This creates special benefits and advantages, since excess volume is not discounted, as it would be in other plans. With most binaries, it is unnecessary to manipulate processing new applications.

CHAPTER THREE

Binary Basics

Why does the binary plan attract so many myths and misconceptions and excite millions of people? The reason is that for years the network marketing axioms, "You build wide for show, but deep for dough" and "Width is money and depth is security," were not obtainable by the masses. The average distributor in network marketing has a hard time just sponsoring three people. But the binary, unlike more traditional plans, is focused on depth rather than width and is fairly easy to understand. If everyone would sponsor just TWO distributors, they could earn commissions! WOW, what a concept!

Once most people grasp an understanding of the binary, they get excited. Some get REAL excited! And when people get excited, they tell other people - - lots of them. The binary plan is truly exciting, and that's why some relatively young companies with binary compensation programs have been among the fastest growing companies in the industry. For that fact alone, you need to understand it and understand it well!

The best way to understand the binary is to know the term "Tracking Center" or "Business Center." I will use the term "Tracking Center," but understand they are one and the same. You will also need to understand that you can ONLY place TWO distributors on your first level (generation) per tracking center. All others you personally sponsor are placed in your downline under one of those two people. The structure now resembles a 2 x matrix, but that is where the similarities end. The binary has no levels or percentages involved in calculating commissions such as those found in the unilevel, matrix, and stair-step break-a-way plans.

Also, only sales volume matters in relationship to commissions, and volume is calculated down the legs in a tracking center as deep as necessary. And in the binary, when the maximum volume amount is reached in a tracking center, the excess volume is breakage; the tracking center starts accumulating again. However, the volume will remain - - month after month until it is commissioned.

In a binary, the volume stop on which commissions are paid in a leg is similar to the break-a-way stop on the number of break-a-way groups. It is also similar to the matrix and unilevel stops that eliminate further commissions at a certain level. However, the binary has no stops on people and no stops on levels. Only the commissionable volume amount is important.

Another reason for excitement in the binary plan is that there is a fair dispersion of income compared to the other plans. Positioning is not "THE IMPORTANT FACTOR FOR SUCCESS" as it is in other plans. By that, I mean the binary doesn't produce a couple of million-dollar top earners (the guys at the top of the plan) while most of the other distributors earn nothing. In binary companies, since successful distributors place new distributors in their downlines, commissionable sales volume is distributed to entire lines of people. As a result, the commissions paid on that volume are spread out more evenly among entire groups of distributors.

That wide distribution of volume is one reason you'll hear about so many people who tried other companies and other plans without much success, but achieved great success with a company using a binary plan - - often with similar products! More distributors are earning commissions than in any other form of distributor compensation and many more reach their levels of success. When this information filters into a matrix, unilevel, or stair-step plan, people jump ship. Why? Because MOST became involved because they wanted to EARN money. If they feel they can earn more money in a binary, they will try!

This is why the binary plan attracts so many myths and misconceptions. People don't like to see their distributors leaving their downlines for another opportunity. This affects their commissions in a negative way.

Remembering that your binary tracking center is divided into two sides: a left and a right, you will first proceed to sponsor two distributors and place one on your left leg and one on your right leg.

The following "TIMELINE" shows the potential of this duplication occurring ONLY once a month for twelve months:

Jan	Feb	Mar	Apr	May	Jun	Jul	Aug	Sep	Oct	Nov	Dec	TOTAL
2	4	8	16	32	64	128	256	512	1024	2048	4096	**8190**

The above is a TIMELINE. If you started your network business in January by sponsoring just 2 people, you would have 2 under Jan. If you worked with these two people for each to sponsor 2 people, you would have 4 under FEB and a total of 6 people in your sales group. Now, if you worked with your first two people to help their two people sponsor 2 each, you would have 8 under MAR and a total of 14 in your sales organization. Then, if you helped these 8 each sponsor 2, you would have 16 under APRIL and a total of 30 in your sales organization.

See how you can grow if everyone made just 2 sales? By the end of ONE calendar year you could have a total of 8,190 people in your sales organization. Now use this to show why your prospect or new distributor should commit to ONE YEAR!

Now if you look at the duplication principle of the above, you will easily see that the binary system is by far the most simple structure ever used in network marketing compensation plans.

POWER LEGS

If you have not heard of this terminology as related to binary compensation structure, you soon will. Basically, a power leg is created by upline members as they each sponsor new distributors and place them in a common leg to benefit distributors in that particular leg. A power leg creates the runaway leg that so many distributors complain about.

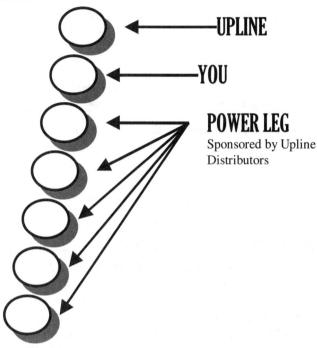

The above illustration shows your tracking center in relationship to your upline sponsor. Your relationship is LEFT SIDE COMMON. Members of your upline placed the tracking centers below your left leg. In other words, they started building and developing "ONE SIDE" of your commission check. You will also place a distributor in the common leg as part of your company's qualification (most companies require you to sponsor a minimum of one distributor on each side of your tracking center). Each distributor below you will also be required to place a distributor in this leg; thus, the common or "Power Leg" will continue to grow and prosper.

Assume that you were capable of sponsoring MORE than two distributors, and you wanted to create power legs to your organization. You would first sponsor two distributors, one left and one right. All other distributors you sponsor would be placed outside left or inside right (depending on your company's computer preference). You would teach your distributors to do the same. When you create half of their sales organizations, they will increase yours by building their other sides. You actually create a reason for each of them to go to work immediately building their opposite legs.

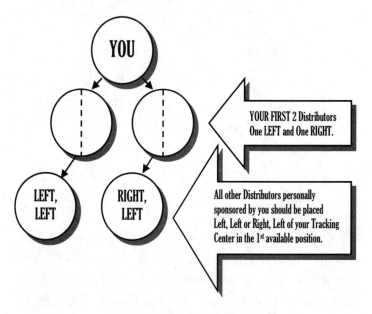

YOU

YOUR FIRST 2 Distributors
One LEFT and One RIGHT.

LEFT,
LEFT

RIGHT,
LEFT

All other Distributors personally sponsored by you should be placed Left, Left or Right, Left of your Tracking Center in the 1st available position.

Suppose you had an organization with twenty-five distributors structured in a power leg on your left leg and twenty-five on your right. When all of these distributors started to work and just sponsored their first two distributors, you would have one hundred new distributors and one hundred sales, fifty left and fifty right!

This is the psychology behind building power legs. Power legs create common leg volume for many distributors. To benefit from this arrangement, all they have to do is go to work building to their non-common legs.

BREAKAGE

Breakage is a term used by many distributors to describe the non-commissioned volume that can pass to the company. Breakage is defined as the commissions left unpaid each month compared to the theoretical maximum of the plan. If a compensation plan pays a maximum of 45% but the actual payout is 35% each month, then the breakage would be 10%. On the surface, one might suggest that breakage is unfair, unethical, or at the very least, misleading; that the plan represents itself as paying 45% but actually pays 35%. Upon closer examination, however, a plan which uses breakage wisely will reward the producers much more generously than one without breakage. It allows a company that can only afford 45% for commissions expense to pay perhaps 10% or more in bonuses to the distributors doing the greatest amount of work. Breakage can be a strong competitive advantage if it is used correctly and for the right reasons.

For example, your pay plan pays on volume matches of $1,000 left and $1,000 right. Each time you match $1,000, you earn $250. You are limited to earning $5,000 each week. The computer program tracking sales for your downline will accumulate up to $10,000 per leg. Any commissionable sales volume in excess of $10,000 will be considered BREAKAGE to you. Because many other people that are linked by sponsorship use the same volume you do to earn commissions, this breakage does not just float to the company as "EXTRA" profit. Rather, it is part of the calculations considered when your company designed its pay plan. However, many companies use some of this breakage in the form of incentive bonuses to reward the distributors doing the best job. If there were no breakage, there would be no additional bonuses.

You will undoubtedly hear many people complaining about the breakage they lose in the plan. What they need to be concerned about is making more sales on their other leg and earning a larger commission check. There will be those distributors who understand the breakage principle yet will still voice complaints about it. They simply need to start their own company and operate it WITHOUT a profit. Then everyone can guess just how long he or she will stay in business - - NOT Long! Breakage is just part of the business and is part of the original calculations involved in designing the distributor compensation program you are working. If you are experiencing breakage that you could have earned on, then it is time for you to work a little harder.

The rumor mills of misconceptions about the binary plan may even be perpetrated by top distributors in other programs who are losing more distributors on a weekly basis to binary plans than any other type of program. Since the binary plan pays on a weekly basis and eliminates problems from "stacking," it will continue to attract the informed networker.

CHAPTER FOUR

Building
By Design

There are several methods that can be used to build a binary organization. One is to start your two distributors, one left and one right, and then help them duplicate. Then focus your efforts on helping all new distributors in your organization to complete this simple duplication and help their own distributors to do the same.

There is also a FAST method that can be used to create an organization in a short time. This is called "Building with Point Contracts." A point contract is the same as the lead horse in a race - - it is the FIRST!

When building with a point contract, you must be ready to go to work as soon as you sponsor your first new distributor; and you must have a good prospect list with phone numbers, ready to call. Here is the way a point contract works:

As soon as you sponsor your first distributor, place his or her application and order form on the left side of your desk. This will be your left leg in your binary tracking center.

Start calling your prospect list. When you have a prospect interested, tell him/her that you have a contract (application and order) on your desk. If he/she joins immediately, you will place this contract underneath on his/her Left side! Now as soon as you have this contract, call your next prospect and say that you have TWO contracts you will place under his/her left side, if he/she joins NOW! As soon as you have this contract, place it on the left side of your desk and call your next prospect. Tell him/her that by joining today, you have THREE contracts you can place under the left leg right now! You can continue this process all week until you have built a good foundation to your left leg. Many networkers work this principle until they have at least ten contracts. When all of these ten people sponsor their first two distributors, you will have thirty distributors in your left leg. Since most binary plans require that distributors personally sponsor one distributor on their left and one distributor on their right, your point contract that you used to place ten contracts ABOVE him/her, will now have ten contracts on his/her left leg. This is power building and it works, if you work it!

As soon as you have completed building a point group on your left leg, start a point contract on your right leg and repeat the same procedure. When you complete this, you will have ten contracts on your right leg that will duplicate to thirty distributors.

Some distributors start two point contracts in the beginning. They place the first point contract on the left side of their desk and the second on the right. Now they alternate left to right, developing the left leg with the right leg. The only problem is holding applications. This is why it is recommended to place only ten contracts above the point contract. You should always strive to turn your contracts into the home office each week. Remember that it is important for your people to receive their products and company information as quickly as possible.

You may want to build with a point contract each week. This way, you won't be holding contracts back. If you hold contracts too long, it will reflect on your company since the rumor will be that they are slow in shipping products. You do not want to be the culprit that starts rumors.

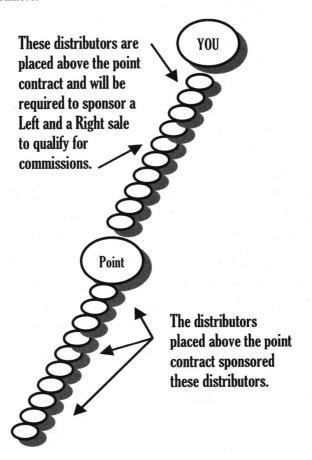

These distributors are placed above the point contract and will be required to sponsor a Left and a Right sale to qualify for commissions.

YOU

Point

The distributors placed above the point contract sponsored these distributors.

CHAPTER FIVE

Multiple Tracking Centers

Your MLM Company may allow you to occupy more than one tracking center. If each tracking center could earn a maximum of $5,000 per week, then three could earn a total of $15,000. Sounds good! Does this work? Well, by the number of people I hear that do not like binaries, multiple tracking centers may be one of the reasons. Now there are certainly some people that CAN build multiple tracking centers, but most people will have their hands full with only one!

If you are capable of building and managing more than one tracking center, then it will be to your advantage to work multiple centers.

There are several configurations of multiple centers, depending on the company. You will find most multiple binary software programs were written to accept Tri-Packs. If you opened three tracking centers and they were structured in a tri-pack, they would look like this:

44

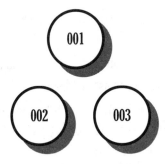

In order to receive three commission checks, you will need to build four legs. You will place your first leg to the left of your 002 tracking center. The second leg should be placed to the left of your 003 tracking center.

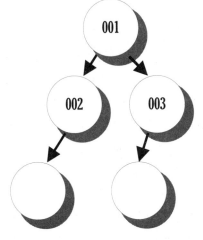

The commissionable sales volume from your 002 leg will accumulate on the left side of your 002 and 001 tracking centers. The commissionable sales volume from your 003 left leg will accumulate on the left side of your 003 and the right side of your 001 tracking centers. When volume matches occur in your 001, you will earn commission checks. The accumulated sales volume will remain in your 002 and 003 tracking centers until you create additional legs

(002 right and 003 right) producing matching volume.

Owning three centers structured in a tri-pack will allow you to build four legs to earn three commission checks, AND you are leveraging the same volume used to earn on your 002 and 003 into your 001! If you were to build three separate tracking centers, you would have to build six legs to earn three checks.

Some companies use a linear or straight line configuration for additional tracking numbers:

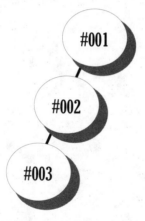

Some call this structure the "String of Pearls." The strength in this structure of multiple centers is that you can build a left and a right leg under your #003 and start earning commission checks in your #003. This sales volume is also accumulated on the left side (whichever side is your common side) of your #002 and #001 tracking centers. Now to earn commission checks in your #002 and #001, you only need to develop one leg Right (whichever is your noncommon side) of #002 and #001 tracking centers!

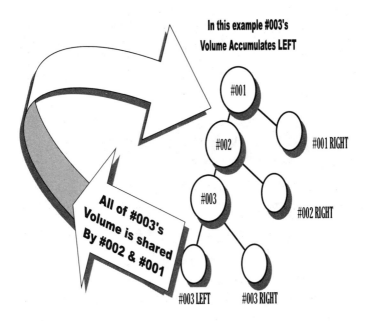

In this example #003's Volume Accumulates LEFT

#001

#001 RIGHT

#002

#002 RIGHT

#003

All of #003's Volume is shared By #002 & #001

#003 LEFT

#003 RIGHT

The binary marketing plan is one of the easiest structures to build and develop if you understand the basics:

1. Each tracking center has two sides.
2. You must build two legs, one left and one right.
3. When the left volume and the right volume match your company's commission increments, you earn a commission check.

CHAPTER SIX

Matching Bonuses

There have been many improvements to the original binary plan that are in use today. One improvement that has a great deal of attraction is the matching bonus. Matching bonuses are based on the weekly (or cyclical) earnings of your personally sponsored distributors.

For example, one company has a plan that allows distributors to earn binary increments of $250 and a maximum earning potential of $5,000 per week. This same company also has a matching bonus program, whereby every distributor who sponsors four distributors can earn a 20% matching bonus based on the binary earnings of their personally sponsored distributors. For instance, if they each earn $250, the sponsor's bonus (above binary earnings) will amount to $200 ($50 each).

This company offers a 40% matching bonus to distributors who personally sponsor ten distributors or make ten sales. So for every $250 that is earned by one of their personally sponsored distributors, the sponsors earn $100.

With ten personally sponsored distributors earning $250 per week, the sponsor will earn a bonus of $1,000 in addition to his/her binary earnings. This is strong improvement and one of the best incentive additions to the binary plan. The matching bonus pays the sponsor additionally for helping his/her people succeed!

The matching bonus can also be a successful sales tool. Say, for example, your prospect has voiced a negative statement about the binary plan yet likes your product. You explain the matching bonus program and that he/she will earn a twenty or forty percent bonus, regardless if he/she earns a binary commission. Explaining the matching bonus may be the turn around point for many prospects opposed to the binary. This allows them to earn matching bonuses without earning a binary commission check.

The matching bonus does place an exciting new twist to an already exciting program, making a matching bonus binary the most significant improvement to network marketing distributor compensation in the last decade.

To sell others effectively on the binary plan, you must know the selling points:

1. The binary plan ONLY requires participants to sponsor TWO

distributors and place one left and one right. Other plans require you to sponsor WIDE to reach depth, and then you are limited only to a few levels.

2. Sales from ALL levels of your organization are accumulated for your commission earnings. Other plans limit your earnings to only a specified number of levels.

3. Binary plans allow you to structure people together that would be placed opposite each other in other plans.

4. There are no hoops to jump through in binary plans. Noncommissioned volume is accumulated until you are paid on it.

5. Multiple tracking centers allow you to leverage work you have already done into additional commissions by developing just one more leg.

6. Binary plans are the easiest for most people to duplicate.

7. Binary plans are straightforward cash machines.

Ultimately, it will not be the binary plan that restricts you in growth; it will be the validity and demand of your product, coupled with your own commitment and desire to succeed.

CHAPTER SIX

The Binary CASH MACHINE

Now that you have a better understanding of the binary compensation plan, you will certainly recognize the advantages of only having to build two legs to earn commissions. You will also agree that all distributors you personally sponsor after your first two will automatically help those that you place them under. You also will have realized that the binary compensation plan is by far the most easily duplicated structure in network marketing. Because of the fact that you can help to build and develop one side of other distributors' tracking centers, the binary is a wonderful structure in which to build a long-term residual income.

The binary compensation plan is by far the fastest building plan in existence due to the fact that you can link leaders to each other, thereby compounding their overall effectiveness and strengths.

Once you understand the binary, you will immediately be bitten by the binary bug and infected for life! Now, let's take a look at some strategies for building and developing your binary organization into

51

a network marketing CASH MACHINE!

You must develop an organized plan of action and outline a strategy for building your organization. This will keep you on track and in profits throughout your journey. Your first strategy is to determine a placement style.

PLACEMENT STRATEGY

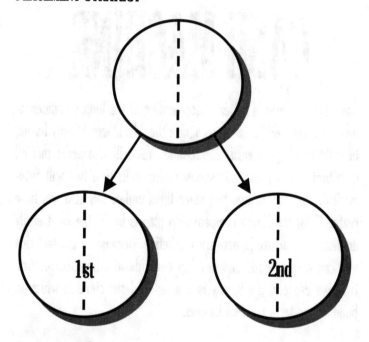

I recommend that you start your first person on your left side and your second person on your right. Now this may seem frivolous; but if you set this pattern and have your distributors follow it also, you all will be on the same page all of the time. With these two following your pattern, your group will start developing.

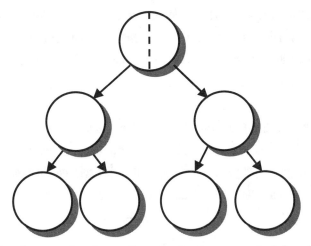

Now that you placed your first two distributors on the left and right of your tracking center, you will be placing all others you personally sponsor under the left or right of your organization. This is where you will want to start the pattern and develop your strategy of placing all those you personally sponsor either on the left, left or the right, left.

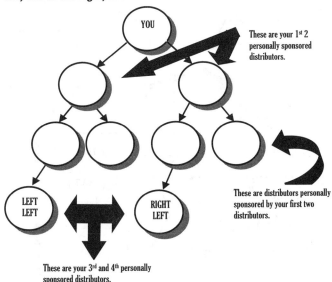

YOU

These are your 1st 2 personally sponsored distributors.

These are distributors personally sponsored by your first two distributors.

LEFT LEFT

RIGHT LEFT

These are your 3rd and 4th personally sponsored distributors.

This strategy not only lets you know where to place the distributors you personally sponsor, but will also tend to create the power legs for your downline distributors. These power legs can help develop commission checks.

By continuing to place your new personally sponsored distributors on the Left, Left and the Right, Left, you can tell other members of your downline that you are building on their left side and they should build on their right. This is true of point contracts as well.

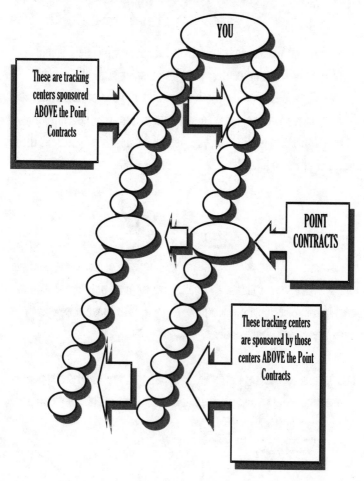

Do you have to place Left, Left and Right, Left? No, the important thing is to be consistent. When you follow this placement structure, tell your distributors that you will be helping on their left and they can place on their right regardless of which leg of yours they may be in.

This is one of the unique traits of the binary compensation plan. You can actually help your distributors by sponsoring new distributors and placing them underneath the older ones without being penalized, as in more conventional plans. This is where the excitement is created in the binary. Imagine many of your upline members placing new distributors in your sales group! How many times does this happen in the more conventional plans?

Suppose you were the 151st tracking center on the Left, and all 150 tracking centers (distributors) above you were placing just one new distributor each month Left, Left; your Left, Left would be increased by 150 new tracking centers!

BUT now, you may have a runaway Left leg. GREAT! Your upline members have just created half of your income. This is not possible in the conventional plans. You now have to build only one leg to get paid. How many legs do you have to build with those other plans to earn the same commissions?

My parting advice to you is: Remember that the binary compensation plan promotes people helping people better than any compensation plan in the industry.

About the Author

Ray H. Duncan is one of Network Marketing's most practiced veterans. He started in the business early working part-time in a multilevel opportunity while attending school. His interest grew as he began to see the monetary growth potential in a plan of people working together to help each other. He continued to work successfully in other MLM programs, and eventually made Network Marketing his full time career.

He has held several corporate positions in the industry and is a consultant to both start-up and established companies.

Mr. Duncan has written numerous Training Manuals and is the author of The MLM ROAD MAP.

Please visit our web site at www.mlmroadmap.com
to purchase additional copies or sales aids.

NOTES: